|插图版|

一个孩子的诗园

［英］罗伯特·路易斯·史蒂文森 著

傅怡 译

陕西新华出版

陕西人民出版社

图书在版编目（CIP）数据

一个孩子的诗园 /（英）罗伯特·路易斯·史蒂文森（Robert Louis Stevenson）著；傅怡译. —— 西安：陕西人民出版社, 2025. 3. —（小书虫读经典）. — ISBN 978-7-224-15555-6

Ⅰ. I561.82

中国国家版本馆CIP数据核字第2024WU4522号

一个孩子的诗园
YIGE HAIZI DE SHIYUAN

作　者	［英］罗伯特·路易斯·史蒂文森
译　者	傅　怡
出版发行	陕西人民出版社
	（西安市北大街147号　邮编：710003）
印　刷	文畅阁印刷有限公司
开　本	787毫米×1092毫米 1/32
印　张	8
字　数	136千字
版　次	2025年3月第1版
印　次	2025年3月第1次印刷
书　号	ISBN 978-7-224-15555-6
定　价	49.00元

如有印装质量问题，请与本社联系调换。电话：029-87205094

世上的东西多如繁星，
我们铁定像国王一样高兴。

——［英］罗伯特·路易斯·史蒂文森

种好处女地
——"小书虫读经典"总序

梅子涵

儿童并不知道什么叫经典。在很多儿童的眼里，你口口声声说的经典也许还没有路边黑黑的店里卖的那些粗制滥造的漫画好看。现在多少儿童的书包里装着的都是那种漫画，还有那些迅速瞎编出来的故事。那些迅速瞎编故事的人都当上富豪了，他们招摇过市、继续瞎编，扩大着自己的富豪王国。很多人都担心呢！我也担心。我们都担心什么呢？我们担心，这会不会使我们的很多孩子成为一个个阅读的"小瘪三"？那么什么叫阅读的"小瘪三"呢？大概的解释就是：没有读到过什么好的文学作品，你让他讲个故事给你听听，他一开口就很认真地讲了一个低俗段子，他讲的时候还兴奋地笑个不停，脸上也有光彩。可是你仔细看看，那些光彩不是金黄的，不是碧绿的，不是鲜红的。那是怎样的呢？你去看看那是怎样的吧，仔细地看看，我不描述了，总之我也描述不好。

所以我们要想办法。很多年来，人类一直在想办法，让儿童们阅读到他们应该阅读的书，阅读那些可以给他们留下美好印象，使他们永远感到温暖，变得善良智慧，懂得生命哲理的书；那些等他们长大以后，能充满留恋地想到、说起，而且心里和神情都很体面的书。是的，体面，这个词很要紧。它不是指涂脂抹粉再出门，当然，需要的脂粉也应该涂抹；它不是指穿着昂贵衣服上街、会客，当然，买得起高价衣服也不错，买不起，那就穿得合身、干干净净。我现在说的体面是指另一种体面。哪一种呢？我想也不用我来解释吧，也许你的解释会比我的更恰当。

人的一生中童年是无比美妙的，也是必须栽培的。如果不把"经典"往这美妙里栽培，这美妙的童年长着长着可能就会弯弯曲曲、怪里怪气了。这个世界实在是不应当有许多怪里怪气、内心可恶的成年人。这个世界所有的让生命活得危险、活得可怜，让很多条道路都不通罗马的原因，几乎都可以从这些坏人的脚印、手印，乃至屁股印里找到证据。让他们不再出现的根本方法究竟是什么，我们目前无法说得清楚，可是我们应该相信，种好处女地，把真正的良种栽入童年这块干净的土地，是幼小生命可以成长，并且可以优质地成长的一个关键前提，是一个每个大人都可以试一试的好处方，甚至是一个经典处方。否则这么多年来世界上各个国家都喊着"经典阅读"简直就是瞎喊了。你觉得这会是瞎喊吗？我觉得不会！当然不会！

我在丹麦的时候，曾经在安徒生的铜像前站立过。他为儿童写过最好的故事，但是他没有成为富豪。铜像的头转向左前方，安徒生的目光如童话般软和、缥缈，那时他当然不会是在想怎么成为一个富豪！陪同我的人说，因为左前方是那时人类的第一个儿童乐园，安徒生的眼睛是在看着那个乐园里的孩子们。他是在看着那处女地。他是不是在想，他写的那些美好、善良的诗和故事究竟能栽种出些什么呢？他好像能肯定，又不能完全确定。但是他对自己说：我还是要继续栽种，因为我是一个种处女地的人！

安徒生铜像软和、缥缈的目光也是哥本哈根大街上的一个童话。

我是一个种处女地的人。所有的为孩子们出版他们最应该阅读的书的人也都是种处女地的人。我们每个人都应当好好种，孩子们也应当好好读。真正的富豪，不是那些瞎编、瞎出烂书的人，而应当是孩子，是我们。只不过这里所说的富豪不是指拥有很多钱的人，而是指拥有生命里的体面、高贵的情怀的人，是指孩子们长大后，怎么看都是一个像样的人，从里到外充满经典气味的人！这不是很容易达到的。但是，阅读经典长大的人会渴望自己达到这种境界的。这种渴望，本身就已经很经典了！

罗伯特·路易斯·史蒂文森
（1850—1894）

《一个孩子的诗园》原版插图

CONTENTS

目 录

1　一个孩子的诗园
A CHILD'S GARDEN OF VERSES

135　独自一人
THE CHILD ALONE

177　花园里的时光
GARDEN DAYS

217　天使
ENVOYS

一个孩子的诗园

A CHILD'S GARDEN OF VERSES

A Child's Garden of Verses 一个孩子的诗园

夏天在床上

冬天，天还黑着我就得起床，
在昏黄的烛光中穿好衣裳。
夏天，却是天还大亮，
我就不得不早早上床。

我只好趴在床上，
看鸟儿们在枝头欢跳，
听大人们的脚步山响，
一阵阵敲打我窗前的街道。

这是多么让人郁闷：
天蓝蓝，光皎皎，
我多想再玩一阵，
却偏偏让我上床睡觉！

Bed in Summer

In winter I get up at night
And dress by yellow candle-light.
In summer quite the other way,
I have to go to bed by day.

I have to go to bed and see
The birds still hopping on the tree,
Or hear the grown-up people's feet
Still going past me in the street.

And does it not seem hard to you,
When all the sky is clear and blue,
And I should like so much to play,
To have to go to bed by day?

A Child's Garden of Verses 一个孩子的诗园

异想

这个想法令人欢畅：
全世界到处都是美味佳肴，
在每一个有基督徒的地方，
孩子们饭前都感恩祈祷。

A Thought

It is very nice to think
The world is full of meat and drink,
With little children saying grace
In every Christian kind of place.

A Child's Garden of Verses 一个孩子的诗园

在海边

我来到海边,
伙伴们给我一把木铲,
让我挖沙滩。

我挖的沙洞像空酒杯,
潮涨潮退,
杯中盛满了海水。

At the Sea-side

When I was down beside the sea
A wooden spade they gave to me
To dig the sandy shore.

My holes were empty like a cup.
In every hole the sea came up,
Till it could come no more.

A Child's Garden of Verses 一个孩子的诗园

夜晚奇思

当妈妈熄了灯,
整夜,整夜,
我都看见人们在阅兵,
像白天一样真切。

军队,皇帝和国王,
全都拿着各种各样的东西,
他们行进得威武雄壮,
白天你从没看到过这种好戏。

Young Night–Thought

All night long and every night,
When my mama puts out the light,
I see the people marching by,
As plain as day before my eye.

Armies and emperor and kings,
All carrying different kinds of things,
And marching in so grand a way,
You never saw the like by day.

就连草坪上的大马戏团,
　　也没演得这么好看;
我看见各种野兽各类人员,
　　全都整整齐齐列队走向前。

一开始,他们的动作有点慢,
　　后来,却越来越行走如风,
我紧挨着行走在他们身边,
　　一直到我们都沉沉入梦。

So fine a show was never seen
At the great circus on the green;
For every kind of beast and man
Is marching in that caravan.

As first they move a little slow,
But still the faster on they go,
And still beside me close I keep
Until we reach the town of Sleep.

A Child's Garden of Verses 一个孩子的诗园

孩子的责任

小孩子应当永远讲实话，
跟人讲话，要礼貌回答，
吃饭时，也要遵守规矩，
这是要尽量做到的基本礼仪。

一个孩子的诗园

Whole Duty of Children

A child should always say what's true
And speak when he is spoken to,
And behave mannerly at table;
At least as far as he is able.

雨

雨儿滴滴答答，漫天飘洒，
　飘进田野，洒入丛林，
　淋湿了孩子们的伞花，
　　还有海船的船身。

Rain

The rain is falling all around,
It falls on field and tree,
It rains on the umbrellas here,
And on the ships at sea.

A Child's Garden of Verses 一个孩子的诗园

海盗的故事

草地上,我们三个小伙伴,
划着篮子这条船在游荡。
春天的风啊,轻轻地拂面,
摇摆的草啊,像起伏的海浪。

今天,我们要往哪里冒险行进?
留心着天气,跟定启明星?
要不,去到非洲,任随船儿指引?
还是去普罗维登斯①、马拉巴②,或者巴比伦③?

---

① 普罗维登斯,美国罗德岛州首府,大西洋海岸重要港口城市,以机器制造、纺织、石油加工、化学、橡胶等工业为主,以珠宝制品、餐具用银器、服饰用品著称。
② 马拉巴,印度地名,该地区有不少不朽的建筑遗迹,当地的菜肴更是久负盛名,被誉为烹饪的奇迹。
③ 巴比伦,这里指古代巴比伦王国的首都巴比伦城,在今伊拉克首都巴格达以南约90公里处。公元前18世纪前半期,古巴比伦王国汉穆拉比王统一两河流域,即以此为国都。

Pirate Story

Three of us afloat in the meadow by the swing,
Three of us abroad in the basket on the lea.
Winds are in the air, they are blowing in the spring,
And waves are on the meadow like the waves there are at sea.

Where shall we adventure, to-day that we're afloat,
Wary of the weather and steering by a star?
Shall it be to Africa, a-steering of the boat,
To Providence, or Babylon or off to Malabar?

A Child's Garden of Verses 一个孩子的诗园

嗨！可是海上开来一艘军舰，
是草地上哞哞直叫的牛群猛攻向前！
快！赶快躲开它们，它们怒气冲天，
啊！园门是港口，花园是海岸。

一个孩子的诗园

Hi! but here's a squadron a-rowing on the sea—
　　Cattle on the meadow a-charging with a roar!
Quick, and we'll escape them, they're as mad as they can be,
　　The wicket is the harbour and the garden is the shore.

A Child's Garden of Verses 一个孩子的诗园

陌生的地方

没有人敢像我一般，
爬到高高的樱桃树顶，
我紧紧地抱住樱桃树干，
眺望着陌生地方的风景。

我看见邻居的花园，
灿烂着许多花朵，
还有更多好玩的地方，
我可从没见过。

我看见奔流的小河泛起涟漪，
倒映着蓝天，就像明镜；
满是灰尘的小路弯弯曲曲，
人们从这里走到另一个小城。

Foreign Lands

Up into the cherry tree
Who should climb but little me?
I held the trunk with both my hands
And looked abroad in foreign lands.

I saw the next door garden lie,
Adorned with flowers, before my eye,
And many pleasant places more
That I had never seen before.

I saw the dimpling river pass
And be the sky's blue looking-glass;
The dusty roads go up and down
With people tramping in to town.

A Child's Garden of Verses 一个孩子的诗园

要是我能找出一棵更高的树来，
　　我就能看得更远，更远，
看到渐渐变宽的小河流入大海，
　　看到它和海中的船只嬉玩做伴。

　　　看到另一头的马路，
　　　　远远地通向仙境，
那里，所有的孩子在下午五点钟吃饱喝足，
　　那里，所有的玩具都活跳欢蹦。

If I could find a higher tree
Farther and farther I should see,
To where the grown-up river slips
Into the sea among the ships,

To where the road on either hand
Lead onward into fairy land,
Where all the children dine at five,
And all the playthings come alive.

A Child's Garden of Verses 一个孩子的诗园

刮风的夜晚

月亮和星星都已隐身，
大风呼呼地吹得来劲，
夜里黑乎乎湿漉漉，
有个人骑马在赶路。
夜深了，灯火都已熄灭，
他为什么还骑着马不停奔跃？

树枝儿啪啪直响，
船儿在海上晃荡，
蹄声低沉又响亮，
飞奔在大路上；
飞一样疾跑过去，
又飞一样往回奔驰。

Windy Nights

Whenever the moon and stars are set,
Whenever the wind is high,
All night long in the dark and wet,
A man goes riding by.
Late in the night when the fires are out,
Why does he gallop and gallop about?

Whenever the trees are crying aloud,
And ships are tossed at sea,
By, on the highway, low and loud,
By at the gallop goes he.
By at the gallop he goes, and then
By he comes back at the gallop again.

A Child's Garden of Verses 一个孩子的诗园

旅行

我就要动身远航,
去到长着金苹果的地方;
去到那里:上面是异国的天空,
下面是鹦鹉岛,横躺在海中,
鲁滨孙孤身一人在造木船,
只有葵花鹦鹉和山羊陪伴;
去到那里:那东方的城市,
沐浴着阳光,向四周延伸几十英里,
城里到处是清真寺和尖塔,
环绕它们的花园里全是细沙,
多彩的货物,来自四方五洲,
悬挂在集市上出售;

Travel

I should like to rise and go
Where the golden apples grow;—
Where below another sky
Parrot islands anchored lie,
And, watched by cockatoos and goats,
Lonely Crusoes building boats;—
Where in sunshine reaching out
Eastern cities, miles about,
Are with mosque and minaret
Among sandy gardens set,
And the rich goods from near and far
Hang for sale in the bazaar;—

A Child's Garden of Verses 一个孩子的诗园

去到那里：万里长城守护的中国，
　一边是扬起沙尘的沙漠，
　　另一边，是喧嚣的城市，
铃声叮叮，鼓声咚咚，人声嘻嘻；
去到那里：烈日炎炎的森林，
宽得像英格兰，高得像尖塔顶，
　到处是猿猴和可可树，
　　还有黑人猎手的小茅屋；
去到那里：满身鳞甲的鳄鱼，
　眨着眼睛，待在尼罗河里，
　　红色的火烈鸟，
把来到眼前的鱼儿一口逮到；
去到那里：到处都是原始森林，
　吃人的老虎在这里栖身，
　它们聚在一起侧耳细听，
　　提防着猎人靠近，
　　　或是望着轿子里，
　颠簸的路人经过林子；

一个孩子的诗园

Where the Great Wall round China goes,
And on one side the desert blows,
And with the voice and bell and drum,
Cities on the other hum;—
Where are forests hot as fire,
Wide as England, tall as a spire,
Full of apes and cocoa-nuts
And the negro hunters' huts;—
Where the knotty crocodile
Lies and blinks in the Nile,
And the red flamingo flies
Hunting fish before his eyes;—
Where in jungles near and far,
Man-devouring tigers are,
Lying close and giving ear
Lest the hunt be drawing near,
Or a comer-by be seen
Swinging in the palanquin;—

A Child's Garden of Verses　一个孩子的诗园

去到那里：荒凉的茫茫沙地间，
矗立着一座古城，渺无人烟，
城里所有的孩子，不论贵族还是平民，
很久很久以前就已长成大人，
街上或屋里没有半个人影，
也没有孩子或是老鼠的一点动静，
当夜色轻轻摇漾，
整个城市看不到一星灯光。
等我长大了，我要去那里
带着我的骆驼队去到那里；
在黑暗中点起火把，
照亮那些尘土飞扬的餐厅；
欣赏墙上的图画，
看英雄们战斗，欢宴；
还在一个角落里，
发现了古埃及儿童的玩具。

Where among the desert sands
Some deserted city stands,
All its children, sweep and prince,
Grown to manhood ages since,
Not a foot in street or house,
Not a stir of child or mouse,
And when kindly falls the night,
In all the town no spark of light.
There I'll come when I'm a man
With a camel caravan;
Light a fire in the gloom
Of some dusty dining-room;
See the pictures on the walls,
Heroes, fights and festivals;
And in a corner find the toys
Of the old Egyptian boys.

歌唱

鸟儿歌唱满是斑点的鸟蛋,
　　还有树林里的鸟窝;
　水手歌唱船上的船缆,
　　和扬帆出海的船舶。

遥远的日本孩子在歌唱,
　西班牙孩子也歌声嘹亮;
风琴,随着琴师的手奏响,
　　在雨中不停地吟唱。

Singing

Of speckled eggs the birdie sings
And nests among the trees;
The sailor sings of ropes and things
In ships upon the seas.

The children sing in far Japan,
The children sing in Spain;
The organ with the organ man
Is singing in the rain.

期待

等我长成大人,
我会非常强大、神气,
我要告诉别的男孩女孩们,
请不要随意碰我的玩具。

Looking Forward

When I am grown to man's estate
I shall be very proud and great,
And tell the other girls and boys
Not to meddle with my toys.

A Child's Garden of Verses 一个孩子的诗园

有趣的游戏

我们用卧室的椅子，
在楼梯上造了只船，
船上塞满了柔软的枕头芯子，
我们就驾船破浪向前。

我们拿来一把锯和几颗钉，
带上装满清水的花园木桶；
汤姆说："哦，瞧我这记性，
还得带上苹果和蛋糕才行。"——
这些就足以保证，
我和汤姆航海到下午五点钟。

A Good Play

We built a ship upon the stairs
All made of the back-bedroom chairs,
And filled it full of soft pillows
To go a-sailing on the billows.

We took a saw and several nails,
And water in the nursery pails;
And Tom said, "Let us also take
An apple and a slice of cake;"—
Which was enough for Tom and me
To go a-sailing on, till tea.

A Child's Garden of Verses 一个孩子的诗园

我们一整天驾着船朝前开，
　　玩得可真是开心；
可惜汤姆摔下来伤了膝盖，
　　就只剩下我独自一人。

We sailed along for days and days,
And had the very best of plays;
But Tom fell out and hurt his knee,
So there was no one left but me.

A Child's Garden of Verses 一个孩子的诗园

小船驶向何方?

深棕色的河流,
金黄色的沙滩。
两岸的树木飞向身后,
小河不停地奔流向前。

绿叶在水上漂摇,
泡沫聚成一座座城堡,
我的小船在游荡漂浮——
哪里才是回家的路?

Where Go the Boats?

Dark brown is the river,
Golden is the sand.
It flows along for ever,
With trees on either hand.

Green leaves a–floating,
Castles of the foam,
Boats of mine a–boating—
Where will all come home?

A Child's Garden of Verses 一个孩子的诗园

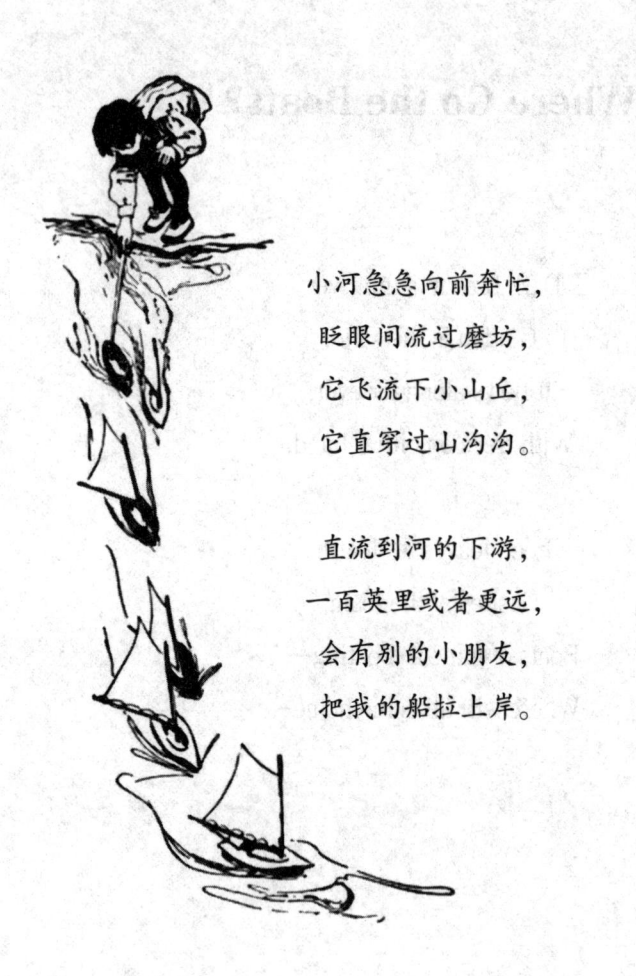

小河急急向前奔忙,
眨眼间流过磨坊,
它飞流下小山丘,
它直穿过山沟沟。

直流到河的下游,
一百英里或者更远,
会有别的小朋友,
把我的船拉上岸。

一个孩子的诗园

On goes the river

And out past the mill,

Away down the valley,

Away down the hill.

Away down the river,

A hundred miles or more,

Other little children

Shall bring my boats ashore.

阿姨的长裙

只要阿姨一走动，
裙子就会发怪声，
跟在身后地板鸣，
滚过房门向前行。

Auntie's Skirts

Whenever Auntie moves around,
Her dresses make a curious sound,
They trail behind her up the floor,
And trundle after through the door.

A Child's Garden of Verses 一个孩子的诗园

床单国

当我生病躺在床上,
我在头下放两个枕头,
所有的玩具都放在身旁,
让我整天都乐悠悠。

有时花个把钟头,
我看着我的铅兵操练,
他们穿着各种制服甲胄,
行动在被褥的山林间;

The Land of Counterpane

When I was sick and lay a-bed,
I had two pillows at my head,
And all my toys beside me lay,
To keep me happy all the day.

And sometimes for an hour or so
I watched my leaden soldiers go,
With different uniforms and drills,
Among the bed-clothes, through the hills;

A Child's Garden of Verses 一个孩子的诗园

有时，我指挥我的舰队，
在床单的大海里劈波斩浪；
或者，我挪开树木和营垒，
建造一座座城市，就在这床上。

我是了不起的好汉，
坐在枕头堆的小山上，
俯瞰着山谷与平原，
做好玩的床单国的国王。

一个孩子的诗园

And sometimes sent my ships in fleets
All up and down among the sheets;
Or brought my trees and houses out,
And planted cities all about.

I was the giant great and still
That sits upon the pillow-hill,
And sees before him, dale and plain,
The pleasant land of counterpane.

A Child's Garden of Verses 一个孩子的诗园

梦乡

白天一整天，从早晨到傍晚，
　　我都和小伙伴待在家里；
每天到了晚上我就离开家园，
　　到遥远的梦乡去游历。

我只能独自去往梦乡，
　　没有人告诉我该怎么办——
我一个人站在溪水旁，
　　或是爬上梦之山。

The Land of Nod

From breakfast on through all the day
At home among my friends I stay,
But every night I go abroad
Afar into the land of Nod.

All by myself I have to go,
With none to tell me what to do—
All alone beside the streams
And up the mountain-sides of dreams.

A Child's Garden of Verses 一个孩子的诗园

稀奇古怪的东西一眼在望,
有的可口,有的漂亮,
还有许多奇异的可怕景象,
直到早晨,一一展现在梦乡。

白天,我怎么努力,
也无法回到梦乡的疆界,
我也记不太起
在梦乡听到的奇妙音乐。

The strangest things are these for me,
Both things to eat and things to see,
And many frightening sights abroad
Till morning in the land of Nod.

Try as I like to find the way,
I never can get back by day,
Nor can remember plain and clear
The curious music that I hear.

我的影子

我有一个小小的影子,我走到哪他就跟到哪,
他有什么用处,我可不知道。
他从头到脚和我几乎分毫不差;
当我跳上床时,他倒比我还先跳。

他是怎么长大的,最是好笑——
一点不像正常的孩子,慢慢长大;
有时他像个弹起的皮球一下子长高,
有时他又变得很小甚至完全找不见他。

My Shadow

I have a little shadow that goes in and out with me,
And what can be the use of him is more than I can see.
He is very, very like me from the heels up to the head;
And I see him jump before me, when I jump into my bed.

The funniest thing about him is the way he likes to grow—
Not at all like proper children, which is always very slow;
For he sometimes shoots up taller like an india-rubber ball,
And he sometimes goes so little that there's none of him at all.

A Child's Garden of Verses 一个孩子的诗园

　　他一点都不知道小孩子喜欢玩什么，
　　　　就会变着法子把我捉弄。
　　他老是躲在我身后，真是胆小得可怜，
　我要是像他黏着我那样缠着保姆我会感到脸红。

　　一天早上，很早很早，太阳还没东升，
　　我起床发现每一朵金凤花上都有露珠闪亮；
　　　　但我懒惰的小影子，像只瞌睡虫，
　　　　　在我身后还死死地睡在床上。

一个孩子的诗园

He hasn't got a notion of how children ought to play,
And can only make a fool of me in every sort of way.
He stays so close behind me, he's a coward you can see;
I'd think shame to stick to nursie as that shadow sticks to me!

One morning, very early, before the sun was up,
I rose and found the shining dew on every buttercup;
But my lazy little shadow, like an arrant sleepy-head,
Had stayed at home behind me and was fast asleep in bed.

规矩

每天晚上我做祷告,
每天白天我就能吃饱;
只要我每天都守规矩,
每顿饭后就能得到一个橙子。

脏兮兮的小孩,
玩具和吃的多得摆不开,
他一定是个不听话的孩子,我保证——
要不,就是他的爸爸糟糕透顶。

System

Every night my prayers I say,
And get my dinner every day;
And every day that I've been good,
I get an orange after food.

The child that is not clean and neat,
With lots of toys and things to eat,
He is a naughty child, I'm sure—
Or else his dear papa is poor.

A Child's Garden of Verses 一个孩子的诗园

乖孩子

天没亮我就醒来,一整天都欢天喜地,
我从不说脏话,只是笑吟吟地玩耍游戏。

现在太阳已落到树林后头,
我很高兴,因为我整天都表现优秀。

我的小床柔软、清爽,
我得上床睡觉,睡前祷告我不会忘。

我知道,明天我会看到初升的太阳,
我不会做噩梦,也没有可怕的梦中景象。

于是我一觉睡到大天亮,
听见画眉在草坪周围的丁香花丛中歌唱。

A Good Boy

I woke before the morning, I was happy all the day,
I never said an ugly word, but smiled and stuck to play.

And now at last the sun is going down behind the wood,
And I am very happy, for I know that I've been good.

My bed is waiting cool and fresh, with linen smooth and fair,
And I must be off to sleepsin-by, and not forget my prayer.

I know that, till to-morrow I shall see the sun arise,
No ugly dream shall fright my mind, no ugly sight my eyes.

But slumber hold me tightly till I waken in the dawn,
And hear the thrushes singing in the lilacs round the lawn.

A Child's Garden of Verses 一个孩子的诗园

睡眠逃兵

客厅和厨房灯火通明,
灯光透出栅栏和百叶窗;
头顶上高高的天空
上万上亿颗星星在闪光。

树叶成千上万,远没有星星多,
教堂里,公园内,人更是少于星星,
成群成群的星星低头望着我,
在黑暗中闪闪发光眨着眼睛。

Escape at Bedtime

The lights from the parlour and kitchen shone out
Through the blinds and the windows and bars;
And high overhead and all moving about,
There were thousands of millions of stars.

There ne'er were such thousands of leaves on a tree,
Nor of people in church or the Park,
As the crowds of the stars that looked down upon me,
And that glittered and winked in the dark.

天狼星，北斗星，猎户星，火星，
还有为水手们海里导航的星星……
挂在天上，闪烁晶莹，
墙边的水桶也盛着半桶水和星星。

大人们最后看见了我，呼喊着追赶我，
转眼就把我放到床上；
星光灿烂，还在我眼里扬起光波，
长长的星河，还在我脑海里荡漾……

一个孩子的诗园

The Dog, and the Plough, and the Hunter, and all,
And the star of the sailor, and Mars,
These shown in the sky, and the pail by the wall
Would be half full of water and stars.

They saw me at last, and they chased me with cries,
And they soon had me packed into bed;
But the glory kept shining and bright in my eyes,
And the stars going round in my head.

A Child's Garden of Verses 一个孩子的诗园

进行曲

弹奏梳子发信号！
冲啊，我们向前！
威利歪戴苏格兰帽，
约翰尼敲鼓声震天。

玛丽·简是总指挥，
彼得统帅后卫营；
列好队，机警而有神威，
人人都是掷弹兵！

Marching Song

Bring the comb and play upon it!
Marching, here we come!
Willie cocks his highland bonnet,
Johnnie beats the drum.

Mary Jane commands the party,
Peter leads the rear;
Feet in time, alert and hearty,
Each a Grenadier!

兵强马壮，威风堂堂，
　快步奔向前方；
　餐巾挂在竿子上，
　一面军旗在飘扬！

赢得了战利品，打了大胜战，
　简真是伟大的统帅！
　围着村庄走了一整圈，
　现在我们应该回家宅。

一个孩子的诗园

All in the most martial manner
　　Marching double-quick;
While the napkin, like a banner,
　　Waves upon the stick!

Here's enough of fame and pillage,
　　Great commander Jane!
Now that we've been round the village,
　　Let's go home again.

A Child's Garden of Verses 一个孩子的诗园

奶牛

温顺的奶牛全身红红白白,
我爱她,全心全意:
她尽心尽力给我牛奶,
就着苹果馅饼真是美滋滋。

她低声哞哞着到处漫游,
她却从来不会迷路,
她在户外清爽的空气里闲遛,
用快乐的阳光把全身洗沐;

任凭风儿阵阵吹刮,
任凭雨儿阵阵淋打,
她悠然自在,不惊不怕,
享用着青青草地上的鲜花。

The Cow

The friendly cow all red and white,
I love with all my heart:
She gives me cream with all her might,
To eat with apple-tart.

She wanders lowing here and there,
And yet she cannot stray,
All in the pleasant open air,
The pleasant light of day;

And blown by all the winds that pass
And wet with all the showers,
She walks among the meadow grass
And eats the meadow flowers.

A Child's Garden of Verses 一个孩子的诗园

快乐的想法

世上的东西多如繁星,
我们铁定像国王一样高兴。

Happy Thought

The world is so full of a number of things,
I'm sure we should all be as happy as kings.

风

我看见你把风筝吹上高空,
我看见你把鸟儿吹向天穹;
我听到你在我周围飞跑,
像女孩的裙子掠过青草——
哦,风啊,你整天不停地吹刮,
哦,风啊,你的歌声传遍天涯!

我看到你做出了许多成绩,
可你总是藏起自己。
我感到你在推我,听见你的啸声,
可我却完全看不到你的踪影——
哦,风啊,你整天不停地吹刮,
哦,风啊,你的歌声传遍天涯!

The Wind

I saw you toss the kites on high
And blow the birds about the sky;
And all around I heard you pass,
Like ladies' skirts across the grass—
O wind, a–blowing all day long,
O wind, that sings so loud a song!

I saw the different things you did,
But always you yourself you hid.
I felt you push, I heard you call,
I could not see yourself at all—
O wind, a–blowing all day long,
O wind, that sings so loud a song!

A Child's Garden of Verses 一个孩子的诗园

哦,你那么强壮而又冰冷,
　　哦,风,你有多大年龄?
你是一只怪兽,活跃在田野和林中,
　　还是一个比我强壮的大顽童?
哦,风啊,你整天不停地吹刮,
　　哦,风啊,你的歌声传遍天涯!

O you that are so strong and cold,
O blower, are you young or old?
Are you a beast of field and tree,
Or just a stronger child than me?
O wind, a-blowing all day long,
O wind, that sings so loud a song!

纪念磨坊

越过边界——无法原谅的罪咎,
我们拨开树枝,向前爬行,
翻过花园墙上的缺口,
我们沿着河岸一路向下冲。

这里是雷鸣轰轰的磨坊,
这里是大坝,翻腾着神奇的浪花,
这里是水闸,流水哗哗奔忙——
多么奇妙的地方,旁边就是我家!

村庄里越来越安静,
山里的鸟儿也静默了歌声;
碾磨工的双眼满是灰尘,模糊不清,
磨的滚动声已使他的两耳变聋。

Keepsake Mill

Over the borders, a sin without pardon,
Breaking the branches and crawling below,
Out through the breach in the wall of the garden,
Down by the banks of the river we go.

Here is a mill with the humming of thunder,
Here is the weir with the wonder of foam,
Here is the sluice with the race running under—
Marvellous places, though handy to home!

Sounds of the village grow stiller and stiller,
Stiller the note of the birds on the hill;
Dusty and dim are the eyes of the miller,
Deaf are his ears with the moil of the mill.

磨坊的轮子碾磨过奔流的岁月,
今天依旧在为我们不停地转动,
它还会永远泡沫四溅,转动不歇,
在我们走了很久之后轰轰雷鸣。

直到我们成了士兵和英雄,
从印度群岛,从海上,回到家乡;
我们仍然发现老磨坊的轮子在转动,
搅动河水,浪花飞扬。

你带着我们吵架时我给你的豆子,
我带着上周六你给我的弹珠,
过去光荣的一切都变成快乐的回忆,
我们把它铭记在心灵深处。

Years may go by, and the wheel in the river
Wheel as it wheels for us, children, to-day,
Wheel and keep roaring and foaming for ever
Long after all of the boys are away.

Home for the Indies and home from the ocean,
Heroes and soldiers we all will come home;
Still we shall find the old mill wheel in motion,
Turning and churning that river to foam.

You with the bean that I gave when we quarrelled,
I with your marble of Saturday last,
Honoured and old and all gaily apparelled,
Here we shall meet and remember the past.

A Child's Garden of Verses 一个孩子的诗园

好孩子和坏孩子

孩子啊,你还太小,
你的骨头还很柔;
你要想长得壮实又健康,
你就得学会走路脚步稳。

你要温顺又快乐,
满足于日常的饮食;
你要远离各种诱惑,
做个天真诚实的孩子。

性情开朗,总是笑吟吟,
在草地上尽情玩乐——
古代的孩子们,
就是这样长成君王和贤哲。

Good and Bad Children

Children, you are very little,
And your bones are very brittle;
If you would grow great and stately,
You must try to walk sedately.

You must still be bright and quiet,
And content with simple diet;
And remain, through all bewildering,
Innocent and honest children.

Happy hearts and happy faces,
Happy play in grassy places—
That was how in ancient ages,
Children grew to kings and sages.

那些坏心肠，没礼貌，
暴饮暴食，吃个不停的孩子，
他们永远别想得到荣耀——
他们完全是另一回事！

坏孩子，流泪包，
长大会变成笨鹅和傻瓜，
随着他们一天天变老，
他们的晚辈个个都憎恨他们。

But the unkind and the unruly,
And the sort who eat unduly,
They must never hope for glory—
Theirs is quite a different story!

Cruel children, crying babies,
All grow up as geese and gabies,
Hated, as their age increases,
By their nephews and their nieces.

A Child's Garden of Verses 一个孩子的诗园

外国儿童

苏族[1]和克劳人[2]的印第安孩子，
寒冷北极的爱斯基摩娃娃，
土耳其和日本的孩子，
喂！你们不羡慕我吗？

你们见过红色的林苑，
见过大海那边的狮子；
你们吃过鸵鸟蛋，
扯过海龟的腿儿。

---

[1] 苏族是北美印第安人中的一个民族，原居北美五大湖以东地区，以从事农业为主。19世纪初，因遭到白人的压迫和屠杀而被迫西迁到大草原，后来又被殖民者赶到南达科他州和北达科他州贫瘠的印第安人保留地生活。
[2] 克劳人又称乌鸦印第安人，属北美大平原印第安民族，生活在黄石河及其支流一带地区，以野牛和马匹为重要生活来源。

Foreign Children

Little Indian, Sioux, or Crow,
Little frosty Eskimo,
Little Turk or Japanee,
Oh! don't you wish that you were me?

You have seen the scarlet trees
And the lions over seas;
You have eaten ostrich eggs,
And turned the turtle off their legs.

A Child's Garden of Verses 一个孩子的诗园

这样的生活真是好,
可是不如我的快乐:
你们天天重复着单调,
厌倦了无法出门远行的生活。

你们吃的是稀奇的东西,
我吃的却是日常的菜饭;
你们只能生活在风浪里,
而我却安全地待在家园。

苏族和克劳人的印第安孩子,
寒冷北极的爱斯基摩娃娃,
土耳其和日本的孩子,
喂!你们不羡慕我吗?

一个孩子的诗园

Such a life is very fine,
But it's not so nice as mine:
You must often as you trod,
Have wearied NOT to be abroad.

You have curious things to eat,
I am fed on proper meat;
You must dwell upon the foam,
But I am safe and live at home.

Little Indian, Sioux or Crow,
Little frosty Eskimo,
Little Turk or Japanee,
Oh! don't you wish that you were me?

A Child's Garden of Verses 一个孩子的诗园

太阳的旅行

晚上睡在床上休息，
太阳公公却还没有空闲；
他还在循着他的轨迹，
一天天不停地绕着地球转。

这里，是晴朗的天空，
我们在阳光灿烂的花园游逛，
而在印度，每个小瞌睡虫，
都被大人吻过后放到床上。

傍晚，我喝完下午茶，
大西洋那边已朝霞初起；
所有西方的孩子啊，
正在起床穿衣。

The Sun's Travels

The sun is not a—bed, when I
At night upon my pillow lie;
Still round the earth his way he takes,
And morning after morning makes.

While here at home, in shining day,
We round the sunny garden play,
Each little Indian sleepy—head
Is being kissed and put to bed.

And when at eve I rise form tea,
Day dawns beyond the Atlantic Sea;
And all the children in the west
Are getting up and being dressed.

A Child's Garden of Verses　一个孩子的诗园

点灯人

我的茶点快好了,太阳也已西沉,
　我从窗口看见李利经过的身影;
每天晚上喝茶的时候你还没坐稳,
　他就拿着提灯扛着梯子沿街点灯。

汤姆想当司机,玛利亚想看海上日月,
　我爸爸是个银行家,有花不完的钱;
可等我长大了,可以选择自己的职业的时候,
　哦,李利,我要跟着你在晚上满大街把灯点燃!

我们很幸运,门前有盏灯,
　他停下来点亮它就像点亮所有灯一般;
你拿着提灯扛着梯子,匆匆前行时;
　哦,李利!今晚请看一眼这个小孩,并冲他点点头!

The Lamplighter

My tea is nearly ready and the sun has left the sky.
It's time to take the window to see Leerie going by;
For every night at teatime and before you take your seat,
With lantern and with ladder he comes posting up the street.

Now Tom would be a driver and Maria go to sea,
And my papa's a banker and as rich as he can be;
But I, when I am stronger and can choose what I'm to do,
O Leerie, I'll go round at night and light the lamps with you!

For we are very lucky, with a lamp before the door,
And Leerie stops to light it as he lights so many more;
And oh! before you hurry by with ladder and with light,
O Leerie, see a little child and nod to him to-night!

A Child's Garden of Verses 一个孩子的诗园

我的床是条小船

我的床啊是条小船；
保姆助我进入船舱；
她给我一身水手打扮，
送我黑夜里驾船启航。

晚上我登上小船，
对岸上的朋友道声晚安；
我闭上双眼，扬帆远航，
什么也不听什么也不看。

一个孩子的诗园

My Bed is a Boat

My bed is like a little boat;
Nurse helps me in when I embark;
She girds me in my sailor's coat
And starts me in the dark.

At night I go on board and say
Good-night to all my friends on shore;
I shut my eyes and sail away
And see and hear no more.

A Child's Garden of Verses 一个孩子的诗园

有时，我像水手一样周到，
　把一些东西放进床里：
也许是一块婚礼蛋糕，
　也许是一两件玩具。

我们整晚在黑暗中泛舟；
　一直开进了白天，
我发现我的船靠着码头，
　已经安全地抵达房间。

And sometimes things to bed I take,
　　As prudent sailors have to do;
Perhaps a slice of wedding-cake,
　　Perhaps a toy or two.

All night across the dark we steer;
　　But when the day returns at last,
Safe in my room beside the pier,
　　I find my vessel fast.

A Child's Garden of Verses 一个孩子的诗园

月亮

月亮的脸像走廊里的钟；
她照着爬到花园墙上的小偷，
照着树杈上的小鸟沉沉入梦，
照着大街，田野和港口的码头。

喵喵叫的猫儿，吱吱叫的老鼠，
屋外门前汪汪叫的狗狗，
整个白天睡懒觉的蝙蝠，
都喜欢在盈盈月光下出来闲遛。

可是喜欢白天的一切，
全都依偎在一起呼呼沉睡；
花朵和孩子们闭眼安歇，
直到早上迎来太阳的光辉。

The Moon

The moon has a face like the clock in the hall;
She shines on thieves on the garden wall,
On streets and fields and harbour quays,
And birdies asleep in the forks of the trees.

The squalling cat and the squeaking mouse,
The howling dog by the door of the house,
The bat that lies in bed at noon,
All love to be out by the light of the moon.

But all of the things that belong to the day
Cuddle to sleep to be out of her way;
And flowers and children close their eyes
Till up in the morning the sun shall arise.

A Child's Garden of Verses 一个孩子的诗园

秋千

你可喜欢荡秋千,
飞身直上蓝晶晶的天?
哦,我觉得这事最好玩,
所有孩子应该都喜欢!

荡过围墙荡上天空,
视野变得无比宽,
我看见河流、树木和牛羊,
田野茫茫无边——

我再低头看,看见绿艳艳的花园,
还有棕色的房顶——
我又荡上蓝天,
荡上落回,在空中反复穿!

The Swing

How do you like to go up in a swing,
    Up in the air so blue?
Oh, I do think it the pleasantest thing
    Ever a child can do!

Up in the air and over the wall,
    Till I can see so wide,
River and trees and cattle and all
    Over the countryside—

Till I look down on the garden green,
    Down on the roof so brown—
Up in the air I go flying again,
    Up in the air and down!

A Child's Garden of Verses 一个孩子的诗园

起床时间

黄嘴巴的小鸟,
在我窗台上跳,
歪着亮晶晶的眼睛闹吵吵:
"懒虫,真不害臊!"

Time to Rise

A birdie with a yellow bill
Hopped upon my window sill,
Cocked his shining eye and said:
"Ain't you 'shamed, you sleepy-head!"

A Child's Garden of Verses 一个孩子的诗园

镜子河

河水静静静静地涌流,
微光闪闪,荡着涟漪——
啊,多么洁净的石头!
啊,多么平静的小溪!

落花漂流,银鱼闪光,
河水像天空一样清澈——
啊,孩子多么希望,
能够住进这闪光的河!

我们看到自己的小花脸,
在摇漾的河水里晃荡。
晃荡在宁静的深渊,
那里又阴又凉;

Looking–glass River

Smooth it glides upon its travel,
Here a wimple, there a gleam—
O the clean gravel!
O the smooth stream!

Sailing blossoms, silver fishes,
Pave pools as clear as air—
How a child wishes
To live down there!

We can see our colored faces
Floating on the shaken pool
Down in cool places,
Dim and very cool;

一阵风来，吹起了水波，
溅湿了貂儿，惊跳了鳟鱼，
涟漪层层远播，
转眼完全消失。

看河面波纹荡漾竞逐高下；
河底像夜晚一样黑暗重重，
就好像妈妈，
吹灭了灯！

耐心点，孩子们，只一会儿——
荡漾的水波就会平静；
溪水和小溪里的一切，
又会变得清澈透明。

Till a wind or water wrinkle,
Dipping marten, plumping trout,
Spreads in a twinkle
And blots all out.

See the rings pursue each other;
All below grows black as night,
Just as if mother
Had blown out the light!

Patience, children, just a minute—
See the spreading circles die;
The stream and all in it
Will clear by–and–by.

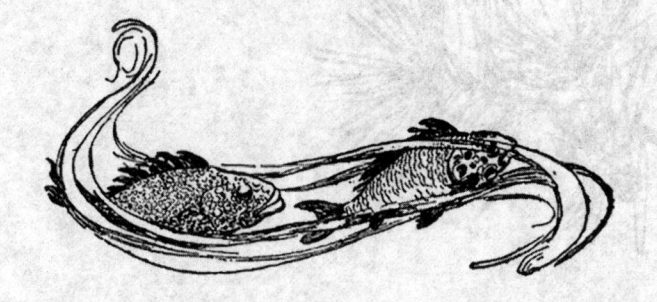

A Child's Garden of Verses 一个孩子的诗园

仙女面包

到这来,脏脚丫!
吃块仙女面包吧。
在我隐居的小屋里,
孩子们,尽情吃,
坐在金黄的扫把上,
安享清凉的松树荫;
等你们全都吃好啦,
一起来讲故事听童话。

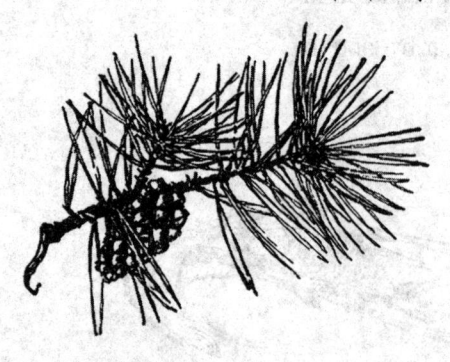

Fairy Bread

Come up here, O dusty feet!
Here is fairy bread to eat.
Here in my retiring room,
Children, you may dine
On the golden smell of broom
And the shade of pine;
And when you have eaten well,
Fairy stories hear and tell.

从火车车厢观望

比精灵还快,比巫婆更急,
穿过桥梁和房屋,穿过篱笆和沟渠;
就像作战的军队,一路冲锋向前进,
穿过草地马群和牛群:
一座座山岭,一片片平原,
像暴雨一样急飞不见;
一次次,眨眼间,
鸣笛驰过花花绿绿的车站。

From a Railway Carriage

Faster than fairies, faster than witches,
Bridges and houses, hedges and ditches;
And charging along like troops in a battle
All through the meadows the horses and cattle:
All of the sights of the hill and the plain
Fly as thick as driving rain;
And ever again, in the wink of an eye,
Painted stations whistle by.

A Child's Garden of Verses 一个孩子的诗园

这里有个小孩爬去爬回,
孤零零地在采摘黑莓;
这里有个流浪汉,站着在张望;
那边有成串成片的雏菊盛开在草场!
这里马路上跑着马车,
载着人,也装满了货;
这里有个磨坊,那边有条小河:
一切转眼就一去不返地闪过!

Here is a child who clambers and scrambles,
All by himself and gathering brambles;
Here is a tramp who stands and gazes;
And here is the green for stringing the daisies!
Here is a cart run away in the road
Lumping along with man and load;
And here is a mill, and there is a river:
Each a glimpse and gone forever!

冬天

冬天的太阳也赖床,
又冷又热的瞌睡虫;
只有一两个钟头闪金光,
然后就像橙子一样血红。

星星还在天空闪烁,
我就起床,在黎明的黑暗里;
光着身子,直打哆嗦,
在冰冷的烛光下洗澡穿衣。

我紧挨着欢乐的炉火坐好,
让我那冻僵的身子回暖;
或是驾着驯鹿坐着雪橇,
去门外更冷的地方探险。

Winter-time

Late lies the wintry sun a-bed,
A frosty, fiery sleepy-head;
Blinks but an hour or two; and then,
A blood-red orange, sets again.

Before the stars have left the skies,
At morning in the dark I rise;
And shivering in my nakedness,
By the cold candle, bathe and dress.

Close by the jolly fire I sit
To warm my frozen bones a bit;
Or with a reindeer-sled, explore
The colder countries round the door.

出门前,保姆把我严严实实
裹在围巾和帽子中,
寒风在脸上火辣辣地痛击,
还夹着雪粒子吹进我的鼻孔。

银色的草地上留下一串黑色的脚印;
大风把我呼出的凉气吹向云霄;
冻住的山岭湖泊,房屋树林,
全都像是大大的婚礼蛋糕。

一个孩子的诗园

When to go out, my nurse doth wrap
　　Me in my comforter and cap;
The cold wind burns my face, and blows
　　Its frosty pepper up my nose.

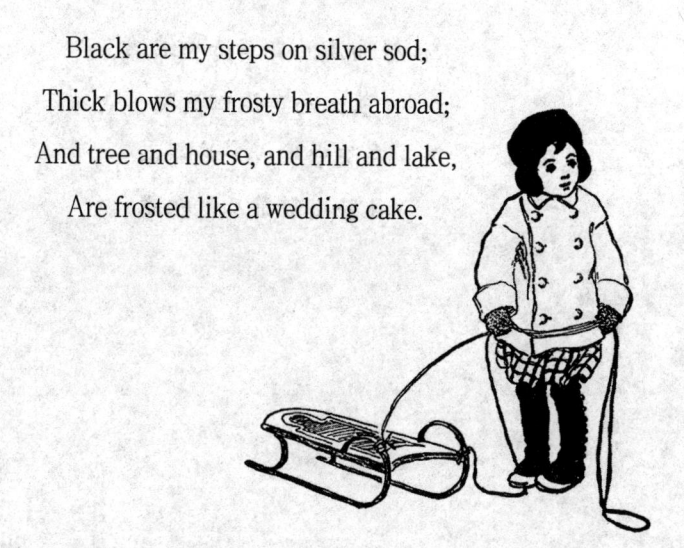

Black are my steps on silver sod;
Thick blows my frosty breath abroad;
And tree and house, and hill and lake,
　　Are frosted like a wedding cake.

A Child's Garden of Verses 一个孩子的诗园

干草棚

令人愉快的整个草场，
　芳草萋萋高过肩膀，
挥动镰刀，银光闪亮，
　遍地割草随地晒晾。

绿油油的青草清香绵绵，
　装上马车运回庭院；
在院中堆成一座高山，
　让登山队员尽情爬攀。

The Hayloft

Through all the pleasant meadow-side
The grass grew shoulder-high,
Till the shining scythes went far and wide
And cut it down to dry.

Those green and sweetly smelling crops
They led in waggons home;
And they piled them here in mountain tops
For mountaineers to roam.

A Child's Garden of Verses　一个孩子的诗园

这里有清凉山，锈钉谷，
那里是老鹰峰和摩天岭——
　　山里住的老鼠，
　　哪会像我这样快乐无穷！

　　啊，爬山多开心，
　　啊，这里真好玩，
空气中满是草香和灰尘，
　　多么快乐的干草山！

Here is Mount Clear, Mount Rusty-Nail,
    Mount Eagle and Mount High;—
The mice that in these mountains dwell,
    No happier are than I!

Oh, what a joy to clamber there,
    Oh, what a place for play,
With the sweet, the dim, the dusty air,
    The happy hills of hay!

A Child's Garden of Verses 一个孩子的诗园

告别农场

接人的马车终于还是来了；
焦急的孩子们赶忙上车，
抛着飞吻，歌声绵绵：
再见，再见，这里的一切啊再见！

再见，房屋和花园，田野和草坪，
还有我们攀爬的牧场大门，
再见，水泵和马棚，大树和秋千，
再见，再见，这里的一切啊再见！

Farewell to the Farm

The coach is at the door at last;
The eager children, mounting fast
And kissing hands, in chorus sing:
Good-bye, good-bye, to everything!

To house and garden, field and lawn,
The meadow-gates we swang upon,
To pump and stable, tree and swing,
Good-bye, good-bye, to everything!

A Child's Garden of Verses 一个孩子的诗园

祝你们永远平安大吉,
哦,干草棚门前的梯子,
哦,干草棚,你结满了蜘蛛网,
再见,再见,这里的一切啊再见!

马鞭声啪啪响起,我们走了;
树和房子渐渐变小;
最后,转过树林歌声飘传:
再见,再见,这里的一切啊再见!

And fare you well for evermore,
O ladder at the hayloft door,
O hayloft where the cobwebs cling,
Good-bye, good-bye, to everything!

Crack goes the whip, and off we go;
The trees and houses smaller grow;
Last, round the woody turn we sing:
Good-bye, good-bye, to everything!

A Child's Garden of Verses 一个孩子的诗园

西北走廊

1. 晚安

屋里点起明亮的灯光,
黑漆漆的时光又开始了;
笼罩着屋外的旷野和小巷,
神怪出没的夜再次回还。

我们看着小小火焰,
它在壁炉里渐渐熄灭了光华,
我们经过时被火光照亮的脸,
就像窗玻璃上的一幅幅油画。

North-west Passage

1. Good-night

Then the bright lamp is carried in,
The sunless hours again begin;
O'er all without, in field and lane,
The haunted night returns again.

Now we behold the embers flee
About the firelit hearth; and see
Our faces painted as we pass,
Like pictures, on the window glass.

A Child's Garden of Verses 一个孩子的诗园

我们真的要上床睡觉？
那么，让我们起身，像大人一样，
勇敢向前胆气豪，
走过黑黑的长廊爬上床。

晚安，哥哥，姐姐，老爸！
晚安，炉火前快乐的伙伴！
晚安，你们的歌声和童话，
晚安，我们明天再见！

Must we to bed indeed?
Well then, Let us arise and go like men,
And face with an undaunted tread
The long black passage up to bed.

Farewell, O brother, sister, sire!
O pleasant party round the fire!
The songs you sing, the tales you tell,
Till far to-morrow, fare you well!

2. 影子游行

房子四周是黑漆漆的夜：
它透过窗上的玻璃往里瞧；
它躲避着灯光，老在墙角里趸，
它随着烛光的移动而奔忙。

我的心像小鼓咚咚狂跳，
随着我头发里妖怪的呼吸；
变形的影子围着蜡烛舞蹈，
沿着楼梯向上跑。

护栏的影子，灯的影子，
小孩子的影子爬上床——
所有淘气的影子都在来来去去，
黑漆漆的夜幕笼上头。

2. Shadow March

All around the house is the jet-black night;
 It stares through the window-pane;
It crawls in the corners, hiding from the light,
 And it moves with the moving flame.

Now my little heart goes a beating like a drum,
 With the breath of the Bogies in my hair;
And all around the candle and the crooked shadows come,
 And go marching along up the stair.

The shadow of the balusters, the shadow of the lamp,
 The shadow of the child that goes to bed—
All the wicked shadows coming tramp, tramp, tramp,
 With the black night overhead.

A Child's Garden of Verses 一个孩子的诗园

3. 在港口

我胆战心惊地飞跑,
我终于走进了卧室,
离开了屋外的幽暗和寒潮,
投入卧室的温暖与关照。

这里一切安全,我们转身,
把跟踪的阴影关在门外,
最后开心地关上房门,
让经历的危险留在门外。

当妈妈去睡觉经过这里,
她会踮着脚轻轻走近小床,
看着我暖暖地躺着休息,
稳妥香甜地快快入梦。

3. In Port

Last, to the chamber where I lie
My fearful footsteps patter nigh,
And come out from the cold and gloom
Into my warm and cheerful room.

There, safe arrived, we turn about
To keep the coming shadows out,
And close the happy door at last
On all the perils that we past.

Then, when mamma goes by to bed,
She shall come in with tip-toe tread,
And see me lying warm and fast
And in the land of Nod at last.

独自一人

THE CHILD ALONE

A Child's Garden of Verses 一个孩子的诗园

看不见的玩伴

当孩子们自个儿在草地上玩,
看不见的玩伴就会来到跟前。
当孩子们快乐、孤独、温顺,
孩子们的玩伴就会走出树林。

没有人听得到他,没有人看得到他,
　他的面容,你永远无法描画,
　但是当孩子们高高兴兴一个人玩,
不论在家里还是在屋外,他一定出现。

他躺在月桂树梢,奔跑在草地上,
你碰响玻璃发出悦耳的叮当声,他就歌唱;
不管什么时候,只要你没来由地满心欢畅,
　孩子们的玩伴就一定在你身旁!

The Unseen Playmate

When children are playing alone on the green,
In comes the playmate that never was seen.
When children are happy and lonely and good,
The Friend of the Children comes out of the wood.

Nobody heard him, and nobody saw,
His is a picture you never could draw,
But he's sure to be present, abroad or at home,
When children are happy and playing alone.

He lies in the laurels, he runs on the grass,
He sings when you tinkle the musical glass;
Whene'er you are happy and cannot tell why,
The Friend of the Children is sure to be by!

A Child's Garden of Verses 一个孩子的诗园

他喜欢细小，讨厌庞大，
　他能在你挖的沙洞里住下；
　　你玩锡兵让两军交锋，
　　　他会带着法国兵永远只败不胜。

　　　当你晚上上床睡觉，
　　他哄你入睡，平息你心潮；
　不管你的玩具躺卧在哪，柜子里或架子上，
他都会独自一人把它们打理照顾好！

独自一人

He loves to be little, he hates to be big,
'Tis he that inhabits the caves that you dig;
'Tis he when you play with your soldiers of tin
That sides with the Frenchmen and never can win.

'Tis he, when at night you go off to your bed,
Bids you go to sleep and not trouble your head;
For wherever they're lying, in cupboard or shelf,
'Tis he will take care of your playthings himself!

A Child's Garden of Verses 一个孩子的诗园

我和我的船

哦,我是这条整洁的小船的船长,
我驾着小船,航行在小小的池塘;
我的小船在池塘里打着圈轻漂;
可是当我长大一点,我就会找到那个法宝,
怎样让我的小船出海远航。

我想小得像玩具水兵一样,
我希望玩具水兵活过来坐在驾驶舱;
让他在身边帮助我,我出海航行,
在水上破浪向前,吹着清凉的风,
我的船儿划呀划呀,奔向前方。

独自一人

My Ship and I

O it's I that am the captain of a tidy little ship,
　　Of a ship that goes a sailing on the pond;
And my ship it keeps a-turning all around and all about;
　　But when I'm a little older, I shall find the secret out
　　　　How to send my vessel sailing on beyond.

For I mean to grow a little as the dolly at the helm,
　　And the dolly I intend to come alive;
And with him beside to help me, it's a-sailing I shall go,
It's a-sailing on the water, when the jolly breezes blow
　　　　And the vessel goes a dive-dive-dive.

A Child's Garden of Verses 一个孩子的诗园

不一会儿你就看见我在急流和芦苇间航行，
你会听到船头破浪的哗哗水声；
玩具水兵陪伴在身边，跟我一起探险远航，
登陆到玩具水兵从未到过的海岛上，
在船头让价值一分钱的大炮轰鸣。

独自一人

O it's then you'll see me sailing through the rushes and the reeds,
    And you'll hear the water singing at the prow;
  For beside the dolly sailor, I'm to voyage and explore,
  To land upon the island where no dolly was before,
    And to fire the penny cannon in the bow.

A Child's Garden of Verses 一个孩子的诗园

我的王国

顺着清亮亮的小溪,
我发现一个小小的森林谷地,
它高不过我的头顶,
到处是石楠花和金雀花,
在夏日里绽放满谷云霞,
有的金灿灿,有的红彤彤。

我把池塘叫作大海;
我把小山坡看成大山脉;
因为我是那么小的孩子。
我造了一条小船,建了一座小城,
我搜寻遍所有的石洞,
一个一个地给它们起名字。

独自一人

My Kingdom

Down by a shining water well
I found a very little dell,
No higher than my head.
The heather and the gorse about
In summer bloom were coming out,
Some yellow and some red.

I called the little pool a sea;
The little hills were big to me;
For I am very small.
I made a boat, I made a town,
I searched the caverns up and down,
And named them one and all.

A Child's Garden of Verses 一个孩子的诗园

我宣布，我主宰这里的一切，
包括天上飞的小麻雀，
还有塘里游的小鲦鱼①。
我是这里的国王；
蜜蜂为我嗡嗡歌唱，
燕子为我翩翩起舞。

这里有最深的海洋，
和最宽广的平原，
我是这里唯一的国王。
最后，到了傍晚，
从屋里传出妈妈的呼唤，
叫我回家吃晚饭。

我只好起身离开我的谷地，
离开我波光粼粼的小溪，
离开我的石楠花丛，
唉！当我走近家门，
我眼前的保姆变成巨人，
房子也那么庞大，那么阴冷！

---

① 鲦（tiáo）鱼，鲤科鱼类，又称白鲦、参鱼、肉条鱼、白漂子。体细长，侧扁，背部几成直线，腹部略凸，头尖，略呈三角形，体背部淡青灰色，体侧及腹部银白色，尾鳍边缘灰黑色，其他鳍均为淡黄色，体长约15厘米。我国南北方各河流、湖泊中有广泛分布，从春至秋常喜群集于近岸水面游泳，行动迅速。

独自一人

And all about was mine, I said,
The little sparrows overhead,
The little minnows too.
This was the world and I was king;
For me the bees came by to sing,
For me the swallows flew.

I played there were no deeper seas,
Nor any wider plains than these,
Nor other kings than me.
At last I heard my mother call
Out from the house at evenfall,
To call me home to tea.

And I must rise and leave my dell,
And leave my dimpled water well,
And leave my heather blooms.
Alas! and as my home I neared,
How very big my nurse appeared.
How great and cool the rooms!

A Child's Garden of Verses 一个孩子的诗园

冬天的连环画

夏天早已远去，冬天降临大地——
　　寒冷的早晨，冻麻的手指，
窗前的知更鸟，冬天的白嘴鸦，
　　还有一本本连环画。

河水变得像石头一样坚硬，
　　我和保姆都能在上面走动；
我们仍能找到流动的小溪，
　　就在那一本本连环画里。

所有漂亮的东西都已画全，
　　就放在孩子们的眼前，
羊儿和牧民，树林和牧羊人的曲柄杖，
　　全都在连环画里装。

Picture-books in Winter

Summer fading, winter comes—
Frosty mornings, tingling thumbs,
Window robins, winter rooks,
And the picture story-books.

Water now is turned to stone
Nurse and I can walk upon;
Still we find the flowing brooks
In the picture story-books.

All the pretty things put by,
Wait upon the children's eye,
Sheep and shepherds, trees and crooks,
In the picture story-books.

A Child's Garden of Verses 一个孩子的诗园

所有的事物,我们都一览无余,
　远近四方的海洋和城市,
　　飞舞着的精灵的面容,
　　　全都在一本本连环画里。

我该怎样歌唱来赞美你?
　这炉火边快乐的日子——
　　安心坐在幼儿室的角落里,
　　　在连环画中迷失自己。

独自一人

We may see how all things are
Seas and cities, near and far,
And the flying fairies' looks,
In the picture story–books.

How am I to sing your praise,
Happy chimney–corner days,
Sitting safe in nursery nooks,
Reading picture story–books?

A Child's Garden of Verses 一个孩子的诗园

我的宝贝

鸟窝后面，藏着我的坚果，
我所有的锡兵也躺在那里休息；
坚果是我和保姆秋天的收获，
就在海边那泉水叮咚的树林里。

我们做的哨子（声音多么美妙！）
那是在场地边缘的田野，
用悬铃木树枝，和我的小刀——
保姆独自帮我把它做好！

独自一人

My Treasures

These nuts, that I keep in the back of the nest,
Where all my tin soldiers are lying at rest,
Were gathered in Autumn by nursie and me
In a wood with a well by the side of the sea.

This whistle we made (and how clearly it sounds!)
By the side of a field at the end of the grounds.
Of a branch of a plane, with a knife of my own,
It was nursie who made it, and nursie alone!

A Child's Garden of Verses 一个孩子的诗园

在不知多远的地方，我们发现一块石头，
　　满身尽是白色、黄色、灰色的花纹；
　　即使又累又冷，我还是把它搬回家门，
虽然爸爸不肯承认，但我认定它是黄金。

我最后一件宝贝堪称"宝贝之王"，
　　很少有孩子拥有这样的奇珍：
　　那是一把有把柄和刀片的凿子，
　　　是一个能工巧匠的作品。

独自一人

> The stone, with the white and the yellow and grey,
> We discovered I cannot tell how far away;
> And I carried it back although weary and cold,
> For though father denies it, I'm sure it is gold.
>
> But of all my treasures the last is the king,
> For there's very few children possess such a thing;
> And that is a chisel, both handle and blade,
> Which a man who was really a carpenter made.

A Child's Garden of Verses 一个孩子的诗园

积木城

你会用积木搭建什么?
寺庙、码头、城堡和宫殿。
让雨一直下吧,让别人去做游客,
我在家玩积木,快乐在心间。

把沙发当作大山,地毯当作海洋,
我为自己建造了一座城市:
城边是磨坊、宫殿和教堂,
还有海港,停靠着我的船只。

宏伟的宫殿,有柱子和围墙,
宫殿顶上再耸立一座塔尖,
楼梯台阶有序地铺装,
直到我的船只平静地停靠在海湾。

Block City

What are you able to build with your blocks?
Castles and palaces, temples and docks.
Rain may keep raining, and others go roam,
But I can be happy and building at home.

Let the sofa be mountains, the carpet be sea,
There I'll establish a city for me:
A kirk and a mill and a palace beside,
And a harbour as well where my vessels may ride.

Great is the palace with pillar and wall,
A sort of a tower on the top of it all,
And steps coming down in an orderly way
To where my toy vessels lie safe in the bay.

这条船在行驶,那条船已停航;
　听,甲板上传来水手的歌声!
　看,国王们在我宫殿的台阶上,
　带着礼物和珍宝在忙个不停!

　　瞧,我建好了。让它去吧!
　　　整个城市哗啦倒地。
　　　一块块积木东倒西歪,
　　还剩什么,我海边的城市?

像以往那样,我又一次见到它,
　教堂和宫殿,船只和居民,
　只要我活着,不论我在哪,
都会把我的海边城市铭记在心。

独自一人

This one is sailing and that one is moored:
Hark to the song of the sailors aboard!
And see, on the steps of my palace, the kings
Coming and going with presents and things!

Now I have done with it, down let it go!
All in a moment the town is laid low.
Block upon block lying scattered and free,
What is there left of my town by the sea?

Yet as I saw it, I see it again,
The kirk and the palace, the ships and the men,
And as long as I live and where'er I may be,
I'll always remember my town by the sea.

A Child's Garden of Verses 一个孩子的诗园

故事书之乡

傍晚,灯已点亮,
爸爸妈妈坐在火炉边;
他们在聊天、歌唱,
什么游戏也不玩。

而我带着木枪,
顺着墙在黑暗中爬行,
就在沙发的后方,
找到了一片森林。

在晚上,没人会发觉,
我躺在猎人的帐篷里,
假扮我读过的故事书中的人物,
直到要上床休息。

独自一人

The Land of Story-books

At evening when the lamp is lit,
Around the fire my parents sit;
They sit at home and talk and sing,
And do not play at anything.

Now, with my little gun, I crawl
All in the dark along the wall,
And follow round the forest track
Away behind the sofa back.

There, in the night, where none can spy,
All in my hunter's camp I lie,
And play at books that I have read
Till it is time to go to bed.

A Child's Garden of Verses 一个孩子的诗园

这里是小山，那里是森林，
这里是星野，荒凉又寂寞；
那里是小河波光粼粼，
咆哮的狮子常来河边解渴。

我看到远处有人影显现，
就好像躺在有灯的帐篷里，
而我就像印第安密探，
悄悄侦察他们的踪迹。

当保姆进来找到我时，
我穿过大海回到家中，
当我上床睡觉时，
还不禁回望我亲爱的故事书之乡。

独自一人

These are the hills, these are the woods,
These are my starry solitudes;
And there the river by whose brink
The roaring lions come to drink.

I see the others far away
As if in firelit camp they lay,
And I, like to an Indian scout,
Around their party prowled about.

So when my nurse comes in for me,
Home I return across the sea,
And go to bed with backward looks
At my dear land of Story-books.

A Child's Garden of Verses 一个孩子的诗园

炉火中的军队

街上的路灯一路闪亮；
落下的脚步轻轻地响；
蓝天慢慢暗淡无光，
夜色笼罩着花园的树木和围墙。

外面现在正下着霜，
红红的炉火照亮了空房：
天花板看起来格外温暖，
书脊上摇曳着闪闪红光。

在火城熊熊的火焰中，
军队经过高楼和尖塔往前冲——
我睁大眼睛仔细观看，
军队消失，光彩暗淡。

独自一人

Armies in the Fire

The lamps now glitter down the street;
Faintly sound the falling feet;
And the blue even slowly falls
About the garden trees and walls.

Now in the falling of the gloom
The red fire paints the empty room:
And warmly on the roof it looks,
And flickers on the back of books.

Armies march by tower and spire
Of cities blazing, in the fire;—
Till as I gaze with staring eyes,
The armies fall, the lustre dies.

A Child's Garden of Verses 一个孩子的诗园

红光重又开始闪耀；
魔幻的城市又熊熊燃烧；
沿着发烫的红色山谷，瞧！
魔幻的军队列队向前跑！

闪光的灰烬，请对我说实话，
这些军队到底要去哪？
你炉子里燃烧着塌毁的火城，
它到底叫作什么名称？

独自一人

Then once again the glow returns;
Again the phantom city burns;
And down the red-hot valley, lo!
The phantom armies marching go!

Blinking embers, tell me true
Where are those armies marching to,
And what the burning city is
That crumbles in your furnaces!

A Child's Garden of Verses 一个孩子的诗园

小人国

我一个人在家坐着,
感到腻味多多,
我只能闭上双眼,
到天空去游玩一番——
漫游到十分遥远的地方,
来到欢乐的游戏之乡;
漫游到遥远的仙境,
那里住着小精灵;
那里三叶草长成大树林,
雨水积成的水洼似海深,
一张张树叶,像一只只小舟,
在水面轻轻漂游;
雏菊上空,
穿过草丛,

独自一人

The Little Land

When at home alone I sit
And am very tired of it,
I have just to shut my eyes
To go sailing through the skies—
To go sailing far away
To the pleasant Land of Play;
To the fairy land afar
Where the Little People are;
Where the clover-tops are trees,
And the rain-pools are the seas,
And the leaves, like little ships,
Sail about on tiny trips;
And above the Daisy tree
Through the grasses,

高高飞过一群大黄蜂,
留下一片嗡嗡。

在那片树林前后左右,
我可以四处游,我可以到处走;
可以看到蜘蛛和苍蝇,
看到蚂蚁排着队前行——
背着东西,抬起小脚,
穿过草坪和长满绿草的街道。
我可以坐在酢浆草里,
瓢虫就在这里栖息。
我可以爬上节节草,
越爬越高,
看见硕大的燕子,
在穿越云霄,
圆圆的太阳慢慢滚过,
一点都没注意到这么小的我。

我穿过那片森林,
直到就像对着一面明镜,
我看见嗡嗡的苍蝇和雏菊,
我看见小小的我自己,

独自一人

High o'erhead the Bumble Bee
Hums and passes.

In that forest to and fro
I can wander, I can go;
See the spider and the fly,
And the ants go marching by,
Carrying parcels with their feet
Down the green and grassy street.
I can in the sorrel sit
Where the ladybird alit.
I can climb the jointed grass
And on high
See the greater swallows pass
In the sky,
And the round sun rolling by
Heeding no such things as I.

Through that forest I can pass
Till, as in a looking-glass,
Humming fly and daisy tree
And my tiny self I see,

被脚下的水洼，
映得清晰如画。
水里的树叶要靠岸，
漂向我站着的地方，
我立马登上这条小船，
环游在这水洼海洋。

体贴的小精灵，
坐在绿茵茵的海滨；
小东西睁着可爱的眼睛，
惊奇地看着我航行。
有些穿着绿色的盔甲
（准是要去武装征伐！）；
有些打扮得五彩纷呈，
黑亮亮红艳艳金灿灿蓝盈盈；
有些拍拍翅膀飞快地掠过；
但他们全都性情温和。

当我重新睁开眼睛，
所有的东西都看得分明：
粉墙高得吓人，地板宽得难受；
抽屉和门上都是巨无霸的把手；

独自一人

Painted very clear and neat
On the rain-pool at my feet.
Should a leaflet come to land
Drifting near to where I stand,
Straight I'll board that tiny boat
Round the rain-pool sea to float.

Little thoughtful creatures sit
On the grassy coasts of it;
Little things with lovely eyes
See me sailing with surprise.
Some are clad in armour green—
(These have sure to battle been!) —
Some are pied with ev'ry hue,
Black and crimson, gold and blue;
Some have wings and swift are gone;—
But they all look kindly on.

When my eyes I once again
Open, and see all things plain:
High bare walls, great bare floor;
Great big knobs on drawer and door;

A Child's Garden of Verses 一个孩子的诗园

椅子上坐着巨人般的大人，
在缝缝补补，引线飞针，
衣服上的皱褶都是我能爬上的小山，
一直没完没了地瞎聊天——
哦，老天，
我的心愿
是做个水手，航行在水洼海洋，
做个登山者，攀爬在三叶草树上，
一直到深夜才回到家中，
趴在床上，睡成瞌睡虫。

独自一人

Great big people perched on chairs,
Stitching tucks and mending tears,
Each a hill that I could climb,
And talking nonsense all the time—
O dear me,
That I could be
A sailor on a the rain-pool sea,
A climber in the clover tree,
And just come back a sleepy-head,
Late at night to go to bed.

花园里的时光

GARDEN DAYS

A Child's Garden of Verses 一个孩子的诗园

黑夜和白天

金灿灿的白天结束了,
大门已经关闭,
孩子和花园,阳光和花朵,
都已销声匿迹。

漆黑的影子缓缓降临,
光线越来越暗,
夜晚的斗篷漫漫飘萦,
一切都沉入黑暗的深渊。

花园昏暗了,雏菊合上花苞,
床上的孩子,都在睡觉——
萤火虫在大路上飞绕,
老鼠们在木堆间窜跳。

Night and Day

When the golden day is done,
Through the closing portal,
Child and garden, flower and sun,
Vanish all things mortal.

As the blinding shadows fall
As the rays diminish,
Under evening's cloak they all
Roll away and vanish.

Garden darkened, daisy shut,
Child in bed, they slumber—
Glow-worm in the hallway rut,
Mice among the lumber.

A Child's Garden of Verses　一个孩子的诗园

　　黑暗中房子亮幽幽,
　　爸爸妈妈拿着蜡烛在走动;
　　可黑夜拧开卧室的门把手,
　　　把一切都变得黑蒙蒙。

　　　终于,黎明飞降,
　　　东方一片火红;
　　　篱笆和荆豆树上,
　　　鸟儿从梦中睡醒。

　　黑暗中所有东西的形状:
　　　房屋,树林,篱笆……
　　渐渐清晰,麻雀展开翅膀,
　　　在窗框上轻轻拍打。

　　这会把打着哈欠的女仆吵醒;
　　　她会打开园门——
　　看见花园里草木上露水盈盈,
　　　清晨已来临。

花园里的时光

In the darkness houses shine,
　　Parents move the candles;
　　Till on all the night divine
　　Turns the bedroom handles.

　　Till at last the day begins
　　In the east a–breaking,
　　In the hedges and the whins
　　Sleeping birds a–waking.

In the darkness shapes of things,
　　Houses, trees and hedges,
Clearer grow; and sparrow's wings
　　Beat on window ledges.

These shall wake the yawning maid;
　　She the door shall open—
　　Finding dew on garden glade
　　And the morning broken.

A Child's Garden of Verses 一个孩子的诗园

我的花园又重绽笑颜,
交织着青草绿和玫瑰红,
奇异得就像昨晚,
它在窗外消失无踪。

昨晚,花园像个玩具,
被锁进了箱子,
现在它沐浴着阳光熠熠,
显得分外亮丽。

每一条小路每一块土地,
每一抹玫瑰的红艳,
每一撇勿忘我的蓝丽,
都有露珠静静躺在那里,

"天亮了,"他们高叫,"快起床!"
我们敲响了晨鼓,
在微笑的山谷上:
"小伙伴啊,快加入我们的队伍!"

There my garden grows again
Green and rosy painted,
As at eve behind the pane
From my eyes it fainted.

Just as it was shut away,
Toy-like, in the even,
Here I see it glow with day
Under glowing heaven.

Every path and every plot,
Every blush of roses,
Every blue forget-me-not
Where the dew reposes,

"Up!" they cry, "the day is come "
On the smiling valleys:
We have beat the morning drum;
"Playmate, join your allies!"

A Child's Garden of Verses 一个孩子的诗园

鸟巢里的蛋

整个夏天,
鸟儿们拍翅唧唧歌唱,
飞舞在花棚一般
月桂树织成的帐篷上。

在月桂树的枝杈,
筑着一个棕色鸟巢;
里面窝着鸟妈妈,
正在孵着四个蓝色的蛋宝宝。

我们站着观测,
像傻瓜一样盯着巢内,
安安稳稳睡在蛋里的,
是鸟妈妈的四个心肝宝贝。

Nest Eggs

Birds all the summer day
Flutter and quarrel
Here in the arbour-like
Tent of the laurel.

Here in the fork
The brown nest is seated;
Four little blue eggs
The mother keeps heated.

While we stand watching her
Staring like gabies,
Safe in each egg are the
Bird's little babies.

A Child's Garden of Verses 一个孩子的诗园

它们很快就会纷纷
啄碎脆薄的蛋壳跳进巢中，
让四月的树林，
充满歌声。

尽管这些雏鸟
比我们幼小更比我们脆弱，
但它们很快就会飞得高高，
成为蓝天的歌唱家和旅行客。

我们，年纪更大，
身子更壮更高，
我们再不能像傻瓜
低头看巢里的小鸟。

花园里的时光

Soon the frail eggs they shall
Chip, and upspringing
Make all the April woods
Merry with singing.

Younger than we are,
O children, and frailer,
Soon in the blue air they'll be,
Singer and sailor.

We, so much older,
Taller and stronger,
We shall look down on the
Birdies no longer.

A Child's Garden of Verses 一个孩子的诗园

它们将歌声嘹亮,
展翅飞向蓝天,
在山毛榉的上方,
高高地盘旋。

尽管我们是万物之灵,
冰雪聪明,妙语连珠,
可我们却只能步行,
用两只脚走路。

花园里的时光

They shall go flying
With musical speeches
High overhead in the
Tops of the beeches.

In spite of our wisdom
And sensible talking,
We on our feet must go
Plodding and walking.

花儿

这些花名是保姆给我的指点：
牧羊人的钱包，园丁的吊袜带，
单身汉的纽扣，小姐的罩衫，
还有蜀葵花太太。

神奇的东西，美妙的仙境，
野蜜蜂飞舞在童话的森林里，
每一棵树下都藏着小精灵——
这些一定都是精灵的名字！

The Flowers

All the names I know from nurse:
Gardener's garters, Shepherd's purse,
Bachelor's buttons, Lady's smock,
And the Lady Hollyhock.

Fairy places, fairy things,
Fairy woods where the wild bee wings,
Tiny trees for tiny dames—
These must all be fairy names!

小小树林的枝叶下面,
精灵在阴暗处织了个房间;
冲着玫瑰或百里香的树巅——
勇敢的精灵正在奋力爬行!

大人们的大树林确实好,
可这里的树林最最奇妙;
要是我不长得这么高,
一辈子住在里面乐逍遥。

花园里的时光

Tiny woods below whose boughs
Shady fairies weave a house;
Tiny tree-tops, rose or thyme,
Where the braver fairies climb!

Fair are grown-up people's trees,
But the fairest woods are these;
Where, if I were not so tall,
I should live for good and all.

A Child's Garden of Verses 一个孩子的诗园

夏天的太阳

伟大的太阳,金光灿灿,
安静地运行在天上;
在天空蓝晶晶的日间,
它洒下比雨丝更密的阳光。

即使我们拉紧百叶窗,
让客厅保持阴暗和凉爽,
它还是能找到一两个细缝,
伸进它那金灿灿的手指。

它钻过锁眼爬进满是灰尘的顶楼,
让结满蛛网的阁楼欢乐闪耀;
它透过瓦片的缺口,
冲架着梯子的干草垛微笑。

Summer Sun

Great is the sun, and wide he goes
Through empty heaven with repose;
And in the blue and glowing days
More thick than rain he showers his rays.

Though closer still the blinds we pull
To keep the shady parlour cool,
Yet he will find a chink or two
To slip his golden fingers through.

The dusty attic spider–clad
He, through the keyhole, maketh glad;
And through the broken edge of tiles
Into the laddered hay–loft smiles.

A Child's Garden of Verses　一个孩子的诗园

　　同时它那金晃晃的脸庞，
　　在花园的每一个地方坦露，
　　　它那温暖又闪亮的目光，
　　　　直透进常春藤深处。

　　　飞过海洋，飞过山河，
　　　它围着亮丽的天空运行，
　　　逗孩子开心，给玫瑰染色，
　　　　它——是宇宙的园丁！

花园里的时光

Meantime his golden face around
He bares to all the garden ground,
And sheds a warm and glittering look
Among the ivy's inmost nook.

Above the hills, along the blue,
Round the bright air with footing true,
To please the child, to paint the rose,
The gardener of the World, he goes.

A Child's Garden of Verses 一个孩子的诗园

哑巴兵

草地已细心地修剪,
我独自一人走在上面,
我在草地上发现一个小洞,
就把一个兵藏进这洞中。

春天飞快赶来,雏菊怒放;
草儿青青遮住了我藏兵的地方;
草儿长成一片绿色的大海,
绿浪滚滚漫过我的膝盖。

他孤零零地躺在草丛下面,
瞪着呆滞的双眼望着天,
红色的制服,尖利的枪,
正对着星星和太阳。

The Dumb Soldier

When the grass was closely mown,
Walking on the lawn alone,
In the turf a hole I found,
And hid a soldier underground.

Spring and daisies came apace;
Grasses hid my hiding place;
Grasses run like a green sea
O'er the lawn up to my knee.

Under grass alone he lies,
Looking up with leaden eyes,
Scarlet coat and pointed gun,
To the stars and to the sun.

A Child's Garden of Verses 一个孩子的诗园

当青草长得像成熟的庄稼一样，
大镰刀再次被磨得锃亮，
当草地又被剃得平整，
就会看见我的小洞。

我会找到他，不必忧心忡忡，
我会找到我的掷弹兵；
可是不管怎样来来去去，
我的士兵都哑默无语。

这个小东西，他栖息
在春天芳草萋萋的树林里；
要是他实话告诉我他的奇遇，
那一定和我想象的相差无几。

他见过繁星满天的夜晚，
看过花儿朵朵绽放笑颜；
他看到过一群群精灵，
嬉戏在森林般的草丛。

When the grass is ripe like grain,
When the scythe is stoned again,
When the lawn is shaven clear,
Then my hole shall reappear.

I shall find him, never fear,
I shall find my grenadier;
But for all that's gone and come,
I shall find my soldier dumb.

He has lived, a little thing,
In the grassy woods of spring;
Done, if he could tell me true,
Just as I should like to do.

He has seen the starry hours
And the springing of the flowers;
And the fairy things that pass
In the forests of the grass.

A Child's Garden of Verses 一个孩子的诗园

万籁俱寂中他听见,
蜜蜂和瓢虫的交谈,
当他独自躺着的时候,
蝴蝶在他头上的草丛漫游。

不管他知道些什么,
他却一个字都不说。
我只好把他放上书架,
自己替他编一个童话。

花园里的时光

In the silence he has heard
Talking bee and ladybird,
And the butterfly has flown
O'er him as he lay alone.

Not a word will he disclose,
Not a word of all he knows.
I must lay him on the shelf,
And make up the tale myself.

秋天的篝火

飘过人家的花园，
飘过山谷上空，
瞧，一缕缕轻烟
升自秋天的篝火边！

快乐的夏天已远逝九霄，
似锦繁花已纷纷凋萎，
红红的篝火熊熊燃烧，
一缕缕青烟随风飘飘。

请歌唱一年四季！
每一季都有自己的风情！
夏天，鲜花遍地，
秋天，篝火熊熊！

Autumn Fires

In the other gardens
And all up the vale,
From the autumn bonfires
See the smoke trail!

Pleasant summer over
And all the summer flowers,
The red fire blazes,
The grey smoke towers.

Sing a song of seasons!
Something bright in all!
Flowers in the summer,
Fires in the fall!

A Child's Garden of Verses 一个孩子的诗园

园 丁

园丁总是沉默不语，
老是让我走石子路堤；
当他放好工具，
就锁上门带走钥匙。

一排红醋栗后的远处——
只有厨师可以去那，
我看见他在奋力挖土，
苍老而严肃，黧黑又高大。

他栽种绿花红花蓝花，
别指望他会搭理你。
他种完花，又去割草，
好像永远都不玩游戏。

The Gardener

The gardener does not love to talk.
He makes me keep the gravel walk;
And when he puts his tools away,
He locks the door and takes the key.

Away behind the currant row,
Where no one else but cook may go,
Far in the plots, I see him dig,
Old and serious, brown and big.

He digs the flowers, green, red, and blue,
Nor wishes to be spoken to.
He digs the flowers and cuts the hay,
And never seems to want to play.

A Child's Garden of Verses 一个孩子的诗园

多傻的园丁！夏天已远走高飞，
　　冬天踮着脚悄悄降临，
　　花园的花草纷纷凋萎，
你只得放下你手里的推车。

　　趁现在还是夏日盛景，
　　趁这收获的黄金时光！
　　哦，你将会变得多么聪明，
　　要是你跟我玩印度人打仗！

花园里的时光

　　　　Silly gardener! summer goes,
　　　And winter comes with pinching toes,
　　　When in the garden bare and brown
　　　You must lay your barrow down.

　　Well now, and while the summer stays,
　　　　To profit by these garden days
　　　O how much wiser you would be
　　　To play at Indian wars with me!

A Child's Garden of Verses 一个孩子的诗园

历史的联想

亲爱的吉姆叔叔,现在你
抽着烟散步的这片园地,
见证了不朽的战绩,
勇士们的血战,有失败也有胜利。

我们最好踮着脚造访,
才能够安全前行,
因为这是有魔法的地方,
谁乱闯谁就会长睡不醒。

这里是大海,这里是沙滩,
这里是淳朴牧人的天地,
这里美丽的蜀葵花争艳,
还有阿里巴巴的岩石。

Historical Associations

Dear Uncle Jim, this garden ground
That now you smoke your pipe around,
　Has seen immortal actions done
　And valiant battles lost and won.

Here we had best on tip-toe tread,
While I for safety march ahead,
　For this is that enchanted ground
　Where all who loiter slumber sound.

Here is the sea, here is the sand,
Here is the simple Shepherd's Land,
　Here are the fairy hollyhocks,
　And there are Ali Baba's rocks.

A Child's Garden of Verses 一个孩子的诗园

但是,瞧那边!远远的高地,
　　是天寒地冻的西伯利亚;
我和威廉·退尔①还有罗伯特·布鲁斯②,
　　在那里受困于魔法师的魔法。

很快,我们就被戴上枷锁,
　　投入寒冷的地牢,漆黑一团;
我们终于站起身来,奋力挣脱,
　　我们的铁镣断裂成两半。

城里所有的号角都呜呜吹响;
　　所有的巨人都跨上战马,
　　　马蹄嘚嘚,刀剑铿锵,
跟在我们身后,跃过金雀花。

---

① 威廉·退尔,瑞士民间传说中的英雄,是14世纪瑞士反对奥地利哈布斯堡王朝统治的自由战士。退尔是一个神箭手,哈布斯堡王朝的重臣盖斯勒强迫他用箭射下他小儿子头上的苹果,他准确地射下了苹果,也射死了盖斯勒,这便成了瑞士人民起义的导火线。
② 罗伯特·布鲁斯(1274—1329),苏格兰历史上重要的国王,他曾经领导苏格兰人打败英格兰人,实现民族独立。他在位期间,政体开明,司法公正,在人民中享有极高的威望。

But yonder, see! apart and high,
Frozen Siberia lies; where I,
With Robert Bruce and William Tell,
Was bound by an enchanter's spell.

There, then, awhile in chains we lay,
In wintry dungeons, far from day;
But ris'n at length, with might and main,
Our iron fetters burst in twain.

Then all the horns were blown in town;
And to the ramparts clanging down,
All the giants leaped to horse
And charged behind us through the gorse.

A Child's Garden of Verses 一个孩子的诗园

　　　　我和伙伴们骑马飞奔，
　　　　跨过青黛的高高山脉，
　　　跨过鞑靼地区强盗出没的森林，
　　　跨过银色的河流，喧嚣的大海。

　　　　我们跃马长驱千万里，
　　　　　冲过女巫的小巷，
　　　　　挥舞刀剑，策马飞驰，
　　　　　驰过山腰，涉过浅滩。

　　最后我们勒住缰绳，三人都疲惫不堪——
　　　　我们从马背跳到草地上，
　　　　刚好是喝下午茶的时间——
　　　站在古巴比伦都城的城门边。

花园里的时光

On we rode, the others and I,
Over the mountains blue, and by
The Silver River, the sounding sea,
And the robber woods of Tartary.

A thousand miles we galloped fast,
And down the witches' lane we passed,
And rode amain, with brandished sword,
Up to the middle, through the ford.

Last we drew rein—a weary three—
Upon the lawn, in time for tea,
And from our steeds alighted down
Before the gates of Babylon.

天使

ENVOYS

给威利和汉丽埃塔

如果有两个人能看到
这些关于昔日美好时光的歌谣，
吟唱我们在屋子和花园里的种种游戏——
我的小兄妹，那只会是你俩没有别人。

你们和我在花园的草地上嬉游，
你们一会儿是国王和王后，
一会儿又变成猎人，士兵，水手，
扮演成千上万种角色，挥洒自由。

天使

To Willie and Henrietta

If two may read aright
These rhymes of old delight
And house and garden play,
You too, my cousins, and you only, may.

You in a garden green
With me were king and queen,
Were hunter, soldier, tar,
And all the thousand things that children are.

A Child's Garden of Verses 一个孩子的诗园

如今，我们端坐在大人的位子，
　　安安静静地休息，
　　从窗户的栅栏里，
看孩子们，我们的继承人游戏。

"岁月永逝。"白发人感慨，
　　语气中深感一切不再；
但是那冲决一切、迅飞疾驰的时间，
　　却把爱留在了人寰。

天使

Now in the elders' seat
We rest with quiet feet,
And from the windowbay
We watch the children, our successors, play.

"Time was," the golden head
Irrevocably said;
But time which one can bind, While flowing fast away,
Leaves love behind.

A Child's Garden of Verses 一个孩子的诗园

致母亲

我的母亲，请您也读读我的诗篇，
　为了对那难忘岁月的爱恋，
　　说不定您会再次听到，
　　　孩子的小脚丫沿着地板飞跑。

To My Mother

You too, my mother, read my rhymes
For love of unforgotten times,
And you may chance to hear once more
The little feet along the floor.

A Child's Garden of Verses 一个孩子的诗园

致阿姨

"我们最崇拜的阿姨"——不只是我,
所有你照顾过的孩子都这样叫——
"真不知其他孩子都怎么过?
没有你,我们的童年该会是什么?"

To Auntie

"Chief of our aunts"—not only I,
But all your dozen of nurselings cry—
"What did the other children do?
And what were childhood, wanting you?"

A Child's Garden of Verses　一个孩子的诗园

致米妮

有张大床的红房间，
只有大人睡在里面；
我和你在的小屋子，
我们俩人躺在一起，
我天真地握住你的手求婚，
希望有一场体面的婚姻；
最好的宽大儿童间，
墙上贴着一张张照片，
还有叶扇张开的百叶窗——
在这房间里醒来，心情欢畅，
听枝繁叶茂的花园摇晃，
在风中沙沙作响——
我们舒舒服服地躺在床边，
看着头顶的一张张照片——

To Minnie

The red room with the giant bed
Where none but elders laid their head;
The little room where you and I
Did for awhile together lie
And, simple, suitor, I your hand
In decent marriage did demand;
The great day nursery, best of all,
With pictures pasted on the wall
And leaves upon the blind—
A pleasant room wherein to wake
And hear the leafy garden shake
And rustle in the wind—
And pleasant there to lie in bed
And see the pictures overhead—

A Child's Garden of Verses 一个孩子的诗园

有塞瓦斯托波尔战争[1],
城墙上大炮张嘴露狰狞,
勇士们攀着云梯爬上城墙,
有疾行的船只,咩咩叫的羊,
快乐的孩子们笑嘻嘻,
蹚过没过脚踝的小溪:
这一切转眼间都烟消云散,
而今牧师的住宅也迥异于当年;
它的面貌已焕然一新,
保护着陌生的一家人。
小河,流过一座又一座磨坊,
穿过我们童年静静的花园;
但是,啊!我们再也不是小孩,
不会再去闸口看河水奔泻下来!
那边依旧挺拔的紫杉树下,
我们缥缈的声音还在空中萦挂,
仿佛我们还在花园里玩耍,

---

[1] 塞瓦斯托波尔位于克里米亚半岛西南端,濒临黑海。曾为俄黑海舰队基地。塞瓦斯托波尔战争指的是1854年9月25日—1855年9月8日,在克里米亚战争期间,俄国军队在塞瓦斯托波尔同英法联军进行的著名防御战。

天使

The wars about Sebastopol,
The grinning guns along the wall,
The daring escalade,
The plunging ships, the bleating sheep,
The happy children ankle-deep
And laughing as they wade:
All these are vanished clean away,
And the old manse is changed to-day;
It wears an altered face
And shields a stranger race.
The river, on from mill to mill,
Flows past our childhood's garden still;
But ah! we children never more
Shall watch it from the water-door!
Below the yew—it still is there—
Our phantom voices haunt the air
As we were still at play,

A Child's Garden of Verses 一个孩子的诗园

  我能听到那叫喊的童音：
  "还有多远啊，到古巴比伦？"
  啊，亲爱的，很远，
  离这里很远，很远，——
  不过，你早已去过更远的地方！
  "我能不能去到那里，用蜡烛照亮？"
  又是老掉牙的调子。
  我不知道——或许你可以——
  但是，孩子们，请听明白，
  啊，那可是一去永不回来！
  毫无疑问，永恒的黎明，
  将会升起在山川平原上空，
  熄灭漫天星光和烛光点点，
  在我们又变年轻之前。

  我跨洋过海，把这些诗句
  投寄给远在印度的你，
  不管远隔千里或万里。
  我们谁都无法忘记
  那印度柜子，

And I can hear them call and say:
"How far is it to Babylon?"
Ah, far enough, my dear,
Far, far enough from here—
Yet you have farther gone!
"Can I get there by candlelight?"
So goes the old refrain.
I do not know—perchance you might—
But only, children, hear it right,
Ah, never to return again!
The eternal dawn, beyond a doubt,
Shall break on hill and plain,
And put all stars and candles out
Ere we be young again.

To you in distant India, these
I send across the seas,
Nor count it far across.
For which of us forget
The Indian cabinets,

A Child's Garden of Verses　一个孩子的诗园

羚羊的骨头，信天翁的长翅[①]，
色彩斑斓的鸟儿和豆子，
小帆船，手镯，念珠，屏风，
一个个神像和神圣的钟，
还有巨大的海螺，发出深沉的嗡嗡！
客厅的地板平展展，
那是温馨可靠的苏格兰海岸；
只要我们爬到椅子上，
就可以看见艳丽的东方！
这可算作天方夜谭；
我依旧在客厅，
米妮就在我头顶
精巧的印度柜子中！
她亲切优雅地笑逐颜开，
给我够不着的书架增光添彩。
亲爱的，请伸出你的小手，
把老朋友的这些歌谣接受。

[①] 信天翁是一种形似海鸥的大海鸟，身披白羽，体长1米多，翅膀展开宽4米以上。长年累月在海洋上空驾风戏浪，像滑翔机在海面翱翔，姿态娴雅，优游自在，偏爱狂风巨浪，不喜欢风平浪静，因为失去了风，它们那现存鸟类中最大的翅膀便会感到飞行困难。

天使

The bones of antelope, the wings of albatross,
The pied and painted birds and beans,
The junks and bangles, beads and screens,
The gods and sacred bells,
And the load-humming, twisted shells!
The level of the parlour floor
Was honest, homely, Scottish shore;
But when we climbed upon a chair,
Behold the gorgeous East was there!
Be this a fable; and behold
Me in the parlour as of old,
And Minnie just above me set
In the quaint Indian cabinet!
Smiling and kind, you grace a shelf
Too high for me to reach myself.
Reach down a hand, my dear, and take
These rhymes for old acquaintance' sake!

A Child's Garden of Verses　一个孩子的诗园

致与我同名的孩子

1

总有一天，这本诗集会送到你手里，
让你用适当的速度阅读，小路易斯·桑切斯，
然后，你会发现，很久以前，你的名字，
被英国书商印在书上，在伦敦人尽皆知。

东方与西方会合在这繁忙的大都市，
英国书商印出了每一个小小的字词；
那时你还太小，不会思想，不会游戏，
遥远的外国人却已在想念你。

是的，当你熟睡在摇篮，英国的每一个角落，
有多少小宝宝手中拿着这本诗册；
在大海的另一边，孩子们在自己家里发问：
"谁是小路易斯，妈妈，能不能告诉我们？"

To My Name–child

1

Some day soon this rhyming volume, if you learn with proper speed,
    Little Louis Sanchez, will be given you to read.
Then you shall discover, that your name was printed down
    By the English printers, long before, in London town.

In the great and busy city where the East and West are met,
    All the little letters did the English printer set;
While you thought of nothing, and were still too young to play,
    Foreign people thought of you in places far away.

Ay, and when you slept, a baby, over all the English lands
    Other little children took the volume in their hands;
Other children questioned, in their homes across the seas:
    Who was little Louis, won't you tell us, mother, please?

2

现在你上完拼写课，放下学习，出去娱乐，
寻找蒙特雷①沙滩上的海藻和贝壳，
看见巨大的鲸鱼骨，被海风掀起的沙子埋葬，
看见小小的鹬鸟，茫茫无边的太平洋。

当海雾把你笼罩，玩耍中请莫忘掉
尽管你还不能读懂诗篇，但别忘记我的嘱咐；
尽管你不曾想谁，可半个世界之外某地，
有人正想蒙特利海滩的路易斯！

---

① 蒙特雷是美国加利福尼亚州西部洛杉矶县的一座城市，位于太平洋海岸，旧金山湾区南方，现为蒙特雷花园城市。这里有连绵的海岸线、梦幻般的迷雾和广阔的大陆、干燥的气候。该地有世界闻名的蒙特利湾水族馆和著名的圆石滩高尔夫球场。

天使

2

Now that you have spelt your lesson, lay it down and go and play,
Seeking shells and seaweed on the sands of Monterey,
Watching all the mighty whalebones, lying buried by the breeze,
Tiny sandpipers, and the huge Pacific seas.

And remember in your playing, as the sea-fog rolls to you,
Long ere you could read it, how I told you what to do;
And that while you thought of no one, nearly half the world away
Some one thought of Louis on the beach of Monterey!

A Child's Garden of Verses 一个孩子的诗园

致读者

就像你妈妈从房间里看见
你在花园的树林间游玩,
如果透过这本书的小窗,
你也定会看见
另一个小孩,在很远很远的地方,
在另一个花园里,玩得正欢。
但是,不要以为你敲敲窗,
轻轻一声呼唤,
那孩子就会听见。
他把心思全放在游戏上,
他听不到,也不会看,
他不会被这本书吸引。

To Any Reader

As from the house your mother sees
You playing round the garden trees,
So you may see, if you will look
Through the windows of this book,
Another child, far, far away,
And in another garden, play.
But do not think you can at all,
By knocking on the window, call
That child to hear you.
He intent is all on his play-business bent.
He does not hear, he will not look,
Nor yet be lured out of this book.

A Child's Garden of Verses 一个孩子的诗园

因为，说实话，很久以前，
他就已经长大，远离家门，
而这只是一个孩子的幻影，
　　在那座花园里飘萦。

天使

For, long ago, the truth to say,
He has grown up and gone away,
And it is but a child of air
That lingers in the garden there.

小书虫读经典